Wolves
and Coyotes

By Rosanna Hansen
Illustrated by Pamela Baldwin Ford

Platt & Munk, Publishers/New York
A Division of Grosset & Dunlap

Many thanks to Dr. Randall Lockwood of the State University of New York at Stony Brook for his invaluable assistance in the preparation of this book.

THE MYTHS ● For thousands of years, men believed wolves were evil, bloodthirsty monsters. During the Middle Ages, people in Europe feared wolves more than any other living creature. They believed that wicked men and women used magic to change themselves into wolves at night. These werewolves, or man-wolves, were thought to roam through the dark night killing people and devouring their flesh and blood.

The same Europeans who believed in werewolves told fairy tales about wolves to their children, and some of these tales are still told today. Everyone has heard about the "Wicked Wolf" who gobbled up Little Red Riding Hood's grandmother, and the "Big Bad Wolf" who hungered for the three little pigs. In *Peter and The Wolf,* a greedy wolf swallowed Peter's little friend, the duck. All these stories and legends tell us that the wolf is a terrible, savage beast.

Today, scientists have made careful studies of the wolf's behavior. They have found the "Wicked Wolf" is not a man-eating monster at all! In fact, there is no proof that a healthy wolf has ever harmed a human in the United States. Scientists of the U.S. Biological Survey studied all the so-called "wolf attacks" on people in this country for 25 years, concluding that not even one was an actual attack by healthy wolves.

Even when people live very close to wolves, the animals do not bother them. At Algonquin Provincial Park in Ontario, Canada, there are many wild wolves. Although thousands of children camp near these wolves each summer, none of them has ever been harmed.

If wolves do not normally attack people, why did the Europeans of long ago make up horrible stories about them? Some of the folktales may have been inspired by the occasional attack of a wolf sick with rabies. There are some records of attacks by rabid wolves, but most of these happened centuries ago in Europe. Because the wolves in North America rarely catch this disease, the chance of a rabid wolf hurting anyone today is very unlikely.

The farmers in Europe had another reason for hating wolves: These animals sometimes stole their sheep and cows. Then, when the farmers heard wolves howling in the woods at night, it was easy for them to imagine that these creatures were terrible demons — and so they made up stories about them.

THE REAL WOLF ● The wolf is the largest wild member of the dog family, the *Canidae*. Its scientific name is *Canis lupus*, which means "dog-wolf." Wild dogs of one kind or another can be found in almost every part of the world. Jackals, dingos, coyotes, and foxes are a few of the other members of this family.

Wolves are actually the ancestors of all domestic dogs. Every size and shape of pet dog now in existence — from tiny terriers to burly sheep-dogs — can trace its family tree back over 10,000 years to an ancestor wolf. During that prehistoric time, early man domesticated wolves and found that these intelligent animals made loyal companions. As thousands of years went by, the early wolf-dogs changed, or evolved, into the many dog breeds we know today.

Strangely enough, many people regard the domestic dog as "man's best friend" but still believe its closest relative, the wolf, is a vicious creature that should be destroyed. Some of these wolf-haters think the wolf is "bad" because it kills other creatures for its food. But the wolf doesn't kill out of any love of killing — it must eat other animals to survive. Like most carnivores (meat-eaters), it has a simple digestive system that requires a large quantity of meat. Pet dogs and cats are carnivores, too, and would also have to kill other animals if they had nothing else to eat. Since the wolf has no one to provide food for it (as pets do), it has no choice in how it lives.

The wolf's closest wild relative in North America is the coyote. Pet dogs, wolves, and coyotes are so closely related that they can — and do — interbreed. Eskimos, for example, have mated their sled-dogs with wolves because they found these crossbreeds to be unusually strong, vigorous animals.

THE SOCIABLE WOLF ● Wolves are extremely social animals. They form strong, long-lasting ties with their mates and are devoted parents. Both a father and mother wolf care for their babies, with eager assistance from the other members of the pack. When wolf pups are only a few weeks old, all the adult wolves in the pack bring them food, babysit for them, and play games with them for hours at a time.

The wolf's sociable nature was first discovered by a scientist named Adolph Murie. During the 1940's, Murie lived in the Alaskan wilderness for two years while he studied a group of Arctic wolves. This study was thought very daring of him, for Murie was the first biologist to live near the "bloodthirsty wolves" in their own environment.

Before Murie's research, biologists had usually studied wolves by examining their dead bodies. They would look at the bumps on a dead animal's skull, for example, or check its stomach to see what it had eaten. No one before had studied how wolves lived their lives.

When Murie began his observations of the wolves, he was amazed at how friendly they acted toward each other. Each time two wolves met, he watched them say hello by licking each other and wagging their tails with pleasure. He saw the adults play games together, nuzzle each other, share their food, have evening "songfests," and take turns caring for their pups.

Murie started to question if any animal with such a friendly nature could be the vicious man-eater that men had claimed. To his delight, he soon discovered that when he approached the wolves, they did nothing more than bark at him. None of them tried to attack or harm him in any way. Once Murie even crawled deep into a wolf den to see the tiny pups inside — while the mother and father wolf stood watching him in alarm. The anxious parents barked at him loudly but didn't threaten or attack — even when Murie left with one of their babies!

When Murie published his discoveries in 1944, the spell of *Little Red Riding Hood* was finally broken. At last, scientists had learned the truth about the wolf. Since 1944, other biologists have followed Murie's example and studied wolves in the wild. They have all confirmed and added to his findings.

WAR AGAINST THE WOLF ● Before the white man came to North America, wolves roamed the continent from southern Mexico to the Arctic Circle. They hunted deer in the forests, followed buffalo herds on the plains, tracked caribou in the snow-capped north. Everywhere except deserts and jungles, wolves made their homes. They lived in harmony with Eskimos and Indian tribes, for these peoples accepted the wolves as part of their world. The wolves, in fact, were much admired by Eskimos and Indians for their courage, strength, and skill at hunting.

When the white settlers arrived here from Europe, they brought with them their hatred of the "Wicked Wolf." In 1648, only ten years after the Pilgrims landed, they agreed to pay hunters a reward, or bounty, for every wolf they killed. Soon other colonists followed their example. Settlers on Long Island, New York, declared in 1663 that "whosoever shall kill a wolf, the head being shown to the town or nailed on a tree, shall have seven bushels of Indian corn."

By the time the West was settled, a great "age of extermination" had begun. Western pioneers made an all-out attack on wolves, coyotes, and other wild animals that threatened their livestock. They hired professional hunters to help them do the job. With great efficiency, these hunters proceeded to trap, poison, snare, or shoot any wolf or coyote they could find. Millions of animals died in the wholesale slaughter.

When this century began, the wolves had been exterminated over most of their range. Only the coyotes, because they were smaller and more adaptable, survived in any number.

Today, of all the United States south of Alaska, only Minnesota has a sizable group of wolves. In the northern forests of that state, about 1,000 of these endangered creatures still survive. A handful of wolves hang on in northern Michigan, as well as about 30 protected wolves on Isle Royale (a national park in Lake Superior). In Alaska, there are as many as 15,000 wolves; in Canada, an estimated 28,000. From virtually all the rest of North America, the once-common wolf has vanished.

THE RED WOLF ● Until recently, there were two types, or species, of North American wolves: the gray wolf *(Canis lupus)* and the red wolf *(Canis rufus)*. The red wolf, the smaller of the two, once ranged throughout the south-central United States. It made its home in southern swamps, coastal thickets, and on the central plains. As it was hunted and its habitat was destroyed, however, the number of red wolves grew smaller. The remaining red wolves mated with coyotes and wild dogs until very few purebred members of this species were left. By the late 1970's, less than a hundred red wolves still survived.

In 1980, the red wolf was officially declared "extinct in the wild." The only true red wolves left today are a few in captivity at zoos and wildlife sanctuaries. To save the red wolf from total extinction as a species, some scientists have begun a program to breed them in captivity. Eventually, the scientists hope to take the offspring of these captive wolves and re-introduce them in the wild.

This breeding program is the red wolf's only hope. If it does not succeed, we may only have a few museum specimens marked "Red Wolf — Extinct" to remind us that this creature ever lived.

THE GRAY WOLF ● The gray wolves that still exist in North America are usually divided into two subgroups, or subspecies, depending on their habitat. They are called timber wolves if they live in wilderness forests, or tundra wolves if they live on treeless arctic plains. Tundra wolves are often white or very light in color, and timber wolves are usually gray or black. Also, tundra wolves tend to be larger in size.

In forested areas, each pack of timber wolves claims a territory of its own. The wolves carefully mark the boundaries of their territory in the same time-honored way a dog leaves its mark at a fire hydrant. These special scent-marks act as a "keep-out" sign for timber wolves from other packs.

Tundra wolves, on the other hand, do not have permanent territories. They need to follow the caribou south when the herds migrate in the fall, so these wolves are on the move too much to establish year-round homes.

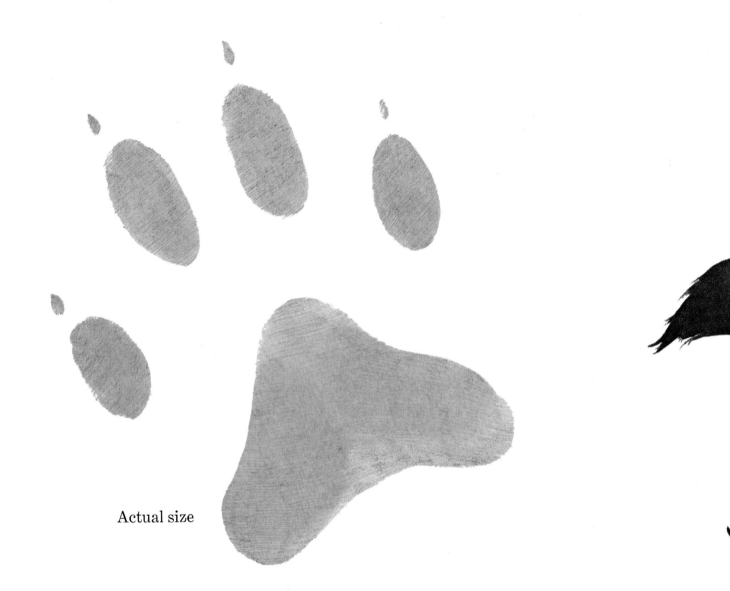

Actual size

WOLF FACTS AND FIGURES ● Suppose for a moment that you are looking at a gray wolf standing beside a German Shepherd dog. At first glance, the wolf would seem like a larger, shaggier version of the German Shepherd. A closer look, though, would show you some important differences. The wolf has a narrower, more graceful body than the German Shepherd, with a smaller chest, larger teeth, bigger paws, and much longer legs.

In fact, the wolf's long, thin legs might be the first thing you would notice. His body is set so high on those skinny legs that he almost looks as though he is standing on stilts. The wolf's big feet act as built-in snow-shoes for him. When he walks on snowdrifts, his toes spread out and keep his weight from sinking down.

The wolf wears a coat of thick, luxurious fur that grows in two layers. The under layer of woolly fluff insulates the wolf's body against the cold. Over this, a covering of long guard hairs sheds rain and keeps the underfur dry.

The further north a wolf lives, the thicker its coat will be. Some tundra wolves have such thick, warm coats that they can curl up in the snow, tails over their faces, and get a good night's sleep at 40 degrees below zero.

In spite of the gray wolf's name, its coat may not be gray at all. Although smoky gray is the most common color for these animals, their fur can also be pure white, jet black, or most colors in between. Some arctic wolves have even had blue-gray coats. Other "gray wolves" have fur that is golden-brown, rust, or light orange in color.

Adult male wolves are usually close to six feet long, including their bushy tails, and average about 80 pounds in weight. Females are roughly half a foot shorter and 5 to 10 pounds lighter. In Alaska, where the largest wolves seem to live, some males have reached a weight of over 170 pounds, with paws that measured a good six inches across.

WAYS OF THE PACK ● Who's top dog? For a wolf pack, that question is vitally important. At the top of every pack is a leader, or "executive" wolf, who makes decisions for the entire group. If the leader guides the pack wisely, all the wolves will benefit — if not, each wolf will suffer. Usually a male wolf is the leader of a pack, though females have been known to take this role.

Within the pack, the wolves maintain a strict social order. There is an "alpha" or top-ranking female who rules the other females, and an alpha male who not only dominates the lower males but is usually the pack leader as well. The lower-ranking wolves treat their leader with great respect and affection. Their loyalty to the executive wolf helps to bind the pack together.

Most wolf packs include a mated pair of adults, their litter of pups, and other adults that usually do not breed. These "extra" adults, who are often related to the mated pair, help them raise the pups. Six to eight wolves is the most common size for a pack, although they have been known to number as many as thirty-six.

As young wolves mature and adults grow older, a pack's social order may change. A younger wolf may successfully challenge the leader for his position; a lower female may replace an aging alpha female. Thus, a wolf's social status can change throughout its lifetime.

To show their social rank, wolves use special gestures and body language. As his badge of office, for example, the leader often lifts his tail higher than the others. His head and ears are held erect, and his proud stance tells you, "I'm in charge here." The lowest-ranking wolf, on the other hand, curls its tail under its legs and holds its ears and head as low as possible when approached by other members of the pack. With its body crouched and eyes cast down, the under-wolf tries its best to avoid any notice.

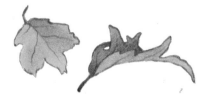

The wolves don't always use body language to show their status, however. When a male leader is courting a female wolf, for example, he may flatten his ears and tuck his tail to show his romantic interest. Also, when the wolves play together, all signs of rank may be abandoned.

When one of the lesser wolves greets the leader, it will whine softly, wag its tail, and lick the leader's face. This is also the way a pup begs for food. By using a puppy's greeting, the lesser wolf tells the leader, "I depend on you, just as a pup depends on its parents."

Sometimes all the wolves greet their leader with a special ceremony. Wagging their tails happily, they rush together and crowd around the leader, while each wolf tries to lick his face or nuzzle him. The leader stands in the midst of this celebration, enjoying the pack's affection.

The wolves may join together in their greeting ceremony when they wake up, before they go out hunting, or when they come home after a hunt. With this ritual, which is often followed by group howling, they express pack unity and show allegiance to their leader.

HUNGRY AS A WOLF ● Wolves rarely know where their next meal is coming from. Although they spend a third of their time in search of food, they often go for days before making a kill. Their stomachs are used to this feast-or-famine life, so the wolves don't feel hunger in the same way humans do. The wolves can even survive for two weeks without eating, if times are hard.

When they do make a kill, the wolves will gorge themselves. They may "wolf down" as much as 20 pounds of meat for one meal. Then, stuffed and sleepy, they often sprawl in the sun for hours to let their food digest.

Wolves have keen senses to help them find their prey. Their sensitive ears, for example, can hear sounds much softer and higher than those heard by humans. Sharpest of all is their sense of smell — at least 100 times more sensitive than man's. The wolf's delicate nose can pick up a scent from over a mile away!

Besides their keen senses, wolves have strong, agile bodies to help them hunt successfully. After they have chased down their quarry, the wolves' long, knife-like front teeth help them seize and hold their prey. Their long front fangs are backed by blade-like teeth that chop and shear meat into chunks.

A hungry wolf will eat almost anything from mice to moose, including rabbits, fish, beaver, and birds. For their main source of food, though, the wolves depend on big animals such as deer, moose, and caribou. These larger animals are hard for the wolves to catch, but they do provide a good dinner once captured. Hunting little animals like mice uses lots of a wolf's energy, and then only serves as a snack.

By itself, a single wolf has little hope of killing a healthy adult caribou, deer, or moose. Besides the advantage of being larger than a wolf, these hooved animals have other powerful defenses. A caribou can easily outrun the fastest wolf, and a moose can kill a wolf with its slashing hooves. So, to overcome these tough opponents, the wolves hunt together as a pack. They sometimes use special group strategies, such as driving their quarry into an ambush, or having some wolves work to distract the prey.

Even with the advantage of the pack, wolves still work very hard for their food. They will stalk and "test" many animals in a herd for each one they actually succeed in killing. Because the healthy prey animals can escape, the wolves single out easy targets: injured, sick, or young animals.

Scientist David Mech once made a study of a wolf pack as it hunted moose. Out of 131 moose that the wolves detected, he found that only 7 were killed. The 124 healthy moose that got away either drove the wolves off with their slashing hooves, or ran so fast the wolves eventually gave up. As Mech said, "These hunts made the famed killers look like amateurs."

This process of selection during the hunt serves an important natural function. By singling out the inferior animals (those that are sick, weak, or young), the wolves help to ensure that only the healthiest prey animals survive. These healthy survivors, in turn, have a better share of the available food and will produce healthier babies. In this way, the wolves actually benefit the species on which they prey and help preserve the balance of nature.

LIFE IN THE FAMILY ● Before her pups are born in the spring, a mother wolf must find a safe home for them. She might choose an underground den, or a cave or hollow log. Usually four to six pups are born, but sometimes — to the mother's great surprise — as many as twelve may appear.

At birth, the pups are short-legged, chubby little balls of fur. They are born blind and are covered with brown, woolly coats to keep them warm. Within two weeks, the babies open their eyes and start to look around the den. During this period when the pups are too young to leave the den, the father wolf will bring food to the mother.

All wolves love pups, so the entire pack is excited when the babies are born. From the first time the pups leave the den, the adults take great delight in them. The father and other adults are eager to start caring for the babies as soon as the mother wolf allows them that honor.

From the pups' point of view, any adult babysitter makes a wonderful rag doll. The little wolves stalk a patient babysitter's tail, chew on its ears, or bite any other handy spot they can get their teeth on. These baby games help the pups develop the hunting skills they will need as adults.

When the young wolves are ready to start eating meat, the adults bring them back food from the hunt. They carry semiliquid meat in their stomachs to the pups and regurgitate it when they reach the den. Because a wolf's stomach is designed to store food this way, the regurgitated meat will arrive as fresh and clean as if it had come straight from a supermarket.

Carrying the pups' food in their stomachs is a very efficient system for the wolves. Since they often have to travel a long way to find food, this method lets them bring large amounts of meat to the pups as easily and as fast as possible.

When the pups spot an adult returning to the den, they rush out to greet it, swarming around the adult while they nip and lick at its mouth. Their eager begging acts as a signal for the adult to feed them. Through the care and affection shown them, the pups learn to love their parents and all the adults. These emotional ties between the young and adults give the pack its unity and strength.

By the time the pups are about eight weeks old, the wolves will move them from the den to a grassy "rest area" close to their main hunting routes. This area makes a safe play headquarters for the pups while the adults go hunting. The pack will move to several of these special areas in the next few months.

The pups are supposed to stay close to the safety of their rest area, but they don't always obey. In his book *Of Wolves and Men,* Barry Lopez tells of a mother wolf who left her pups in their rest area and set off to go hunting. Once she was out of sight, however, she lay down to watch the trail she had taken. A few minutes later, one of her pups trotted merrily over a rise in the path, only to find himself face to face with his mother. The wandering pup "stopped short, looked about as though preoccupied with something else, then . . . began to edge back the way he had come." The mother accompanied him to the rest area and then left for the hunt, this time not bothering to look back. Apparently, she only needed to make her point once, for all the pups stayed where they were supposed to until she returned that evening.

Most of the time, the pups are too busy playing games to think of wandering off. As they play, they practice skills they will need to survive as adults. Hunting, for example, is something the little wolves learn through playing and imitating the adults. From an early age they will practice stalking and pouncing on bugs, mice, adult wolves — and each other. Later, when they start to hunt with the adults, they will learn how to surround their prey, to ambush, and other vital strategies.

By their first birthday, the pups are nearly grown. Some of them will soon go off to find their own territories, while others will stay with the pack.

VOICE OF THE WOLF ● The "wild, untamed music . . . echoed from the hillsides and filled the valleys. It sent a queer shivering feeling along my spine . . . a sort of tingling." With these words, Alaskan trapper Alda Orton described the eerie song of the wolf. Others have compared the wolf's voice to a "low, mournful moan" or even to a "lonesome, sentimental fire engine," but everyone agrees on one thing. The sound, once heard, is never forgotten.

Wolves will howl as a social ritual, to call the pack together, to find each other in strange country, and to announce their territory boundaries to intruding wolves. Also, if a wolf feels lonely, it may show its unhappiness with a special "lonesome" howl.

When all the wolves join in a pack chorus, the results are spectacular. One wolf begins and the others quickly join in, each one choosing a different note. Some of the wolves will yodel and slide from pitch to pitch, creating chords that can be heard up to four miles away.

Wolves will howl in answer to some very unwolflike sounds. A fire siren, for example, often starts them singing, as does a distant train whistle. One wolf expert has found that wolves will eagerly respond to his tapes of grand opera and of U.S. Marine trumpet calls.

At Algonquin Provincial Park in Canada, the sociable wolves will even answer human "howls." Thousands of people visit the park each autumn just to howl with the wolves. Because there is a large population of wolves in this park, the chances of finding a wolf pack and howling with them are very good. No one knows what the wolves think of these song-fests, but the humans have a wonderful time.

Howling is by no means the wolves' only form of speech. They also communicate with barks, growls, squeaks, and whimpers. If a stranger intrudes on a pack's territory, for example, the wolves will bark in warning. Similarly, they will growl to show anger or to threaten another animal.

The wolves' most intimate sounds are their soft, mouselike squeaks. Adult wolves utter these high-pitched sounds when they feed their pups or call to them, and they also squeak softly to each other as a friendly greeting.

TIME FOR FUN ● Did you know wolves and humans play the same kinds of games? Tag, hide-and-seek, tug-of-war, and keep away — these are just a few of the games wolves like to play.

When a wolf feels playful, it will invite its friends to romp by making a special "play-bow." It will stretch out its body, place its front legs flat on the ground, arch its back, wag its tail, grin happily, and then turn and run away. (You may have seen a pet dog make a similar play invitation.)

Usually the other wolves can't resist an invitation to play and will rush to join the fun. They may chase each other in a game of tag, slide down snowbanks together, play keep away with bones or sticks, or have a mock battle. One of their favorite games is "ambush." In this game, one wolf jumps out from a hiding place to scare another, or pounces on a peacefully sleeping wolf.

Many kinds of animals like to play when they are young, but their playfulness usually stops as they grow up. Scientists have found that only the most intelligent animals (such as wolves, coyotes, chimpanzees, and otters) continue to be playful as adults.

Sometimes wolves even play a special game with ravens. Ravens are large crowlike birds that often travel with a wolf pack. Especially in winter, groups of ravens can be seen with wolves, feeding on the remains of their food kills. Through hunting together, the ravens and wolves have developed a social relationship and seem to like each other's company.

Several scientists have seen these two species play a form of tag together. A raven will fly down at a wolf, and the wolf will duck and then leap playfully at it. The bird will fly a few feet in the air and then drop back down for another dive. Both the wolf and the raven seem to thoroughly enjoy this game.

CAN THE WOLF SURVIVE? ● Over the last 20 years, as the wolf population has grown smaller and smaller, some people have become committed to the preservation of these intelligent, beautiful animals. For them, the wolf has become a symbol of the unspoiled wilderness — of all that is wild and free.

Unfortunately, not everyone feels the same way. Other people still believe wolves are "bad" animals, murderers that slaughter innocent creatures. They do not understand that herds of deer, caribou, and moose actually benefit from their relationship with wolves.

Today, after years of struggle between the people who admire wolves and those who hate them, the wolf has finally been granted legal protection in the United States south of Alaska and in the Canadian national parks. But legal protection by itself will not ensure the wolf's survival. The wilderness, too, must be preserved, for without it, the wolf cannot live. Unlike coyotes and other animals that adapt to civilization, the wolf will always be a creature of the wild. If the few wilderness regions where it now exists are changed or spoiled, the wolf will continue to decline.

Will the wolf survive? Only if people believe that it should, and work to protect it and its habitat. As scientist David Mech has said, "The wolf is neither man's competitor nor his enemy. He is a fellow creature with whom the earth must be shared."

COYOTES ● To the Indians of the American West, the coyote was a powerful, sacred animal. The Crow Indians believed that "Old Man Coyote" had created the earth and all living creatures — including human beings. To the Navajos, the coyote was "God's dog." They considered the coyote more important than the wolf, which they simply called "big coyote."

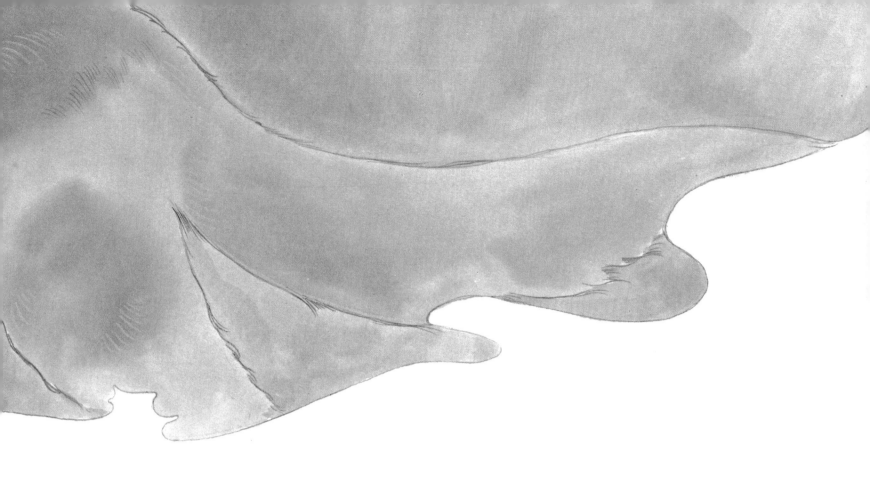

Another Indian tribe believed that at the end of time, the coyote would find a way to be the last animal left on earth. The Indians who told this legend knew the coyote well, for this clever animal has an amazing instinct for survival. Unlike wolves, coyotes have adapted to man's civilization. They have learned to live close to people, and can even survive in our towns and cities. Today, about 2,000 coyotes make their homes within the city limits of Los Angeles. Sometimes these bold urban dwellers can be seen drinking from people's swimming pools. At night, the coyotes often come out to serenade the movie stars in Beverly Hills.

Just as it has learned to live in cities, the adaptable coyote can change its lifestyle in many other ways. It can hunt alone or in pairs, eat anything from meat to melons, raise its pups in an alleyway or in a wilderness den, broil in desert heat or survive an Arctic winter.

Lucky for the coyote that it is so adaptable or it would probably not have survived man's efforts to exterminate it. While the wolf has almost vanished from this continent, the coyote has actually managed to extend its range. It can now be found from Alaska down to Costa Rica, and from California east to New England.

COYOTE FACTS AND FIGURES ● The coyote is a member of the dog family *(Canidae)*, and is the wolf's closest wild relative in North America. Because these two species are so much alike, a coyote can easily be confused with a wolf. Early settlers in the West, for example, believed that coyotes actually were small wolves, and called them "prairie wolves." Today, biologists classify the coyote as a separate species. Its scientific name is *Canis latrans*, or "barking dog."

One important way that coyotes differ from wolves is in size. Although a big coyote sometimes reaches the size of a little wolf, most coyotes are smaller than wolves. On the average, coyotes measure about one-third the size of their larger cousins. An adult male coyote usually weighs around 25 pounds and stands about two feet high at the shoulder. Coyotes also have smaller feet and skinnier legs than wolves, bigger ears, and longer, narrower noses.

The coyote's coat is a tawny color tipped with gray and rust. Its thick, bushy tail has a dark tip and dark spot halfway down the upper side. If it lives in a desert area, the coyote's fur will be lighter and grayer than if it lives in the forest. The lighter colors help the desert coyote blend more easily into its sandy habitat.

Like the wolf, the coyote is highly intelligent and endowed with keen hearing, sight, and sense of smell. Some scientists believe the coyote's hearing is actually ultrasonic, to help it locate the ultra-high squeaks of mice in their burrows.

Besides their physical similarities, coyotes and wolves also act much the same. Like wolves, coyotes generally form long-lasting bonds with their mates and are devoted parents to their young. And, though coyotes don't usually hunt in packs, they do form close social ties with other members of their species. They may live together in groups or clans, and defend their territory against strange coyotes.

Wolves and coyotes use similar body language, too. Both species wag their tails to show pleasure, bare their teeth to threaten, and tuck their tails between their legs to show fear or submission. Also, the coyote is the equal of any wolf when it comes to vocal ability. Its haunting song, complete with trills and tremolos, has become a symbol of the American West.

A MATTER OF TASTE ● The cowboys of the old West used to say, "A coyote will eat anything that doesn't eat it first." That saying is close to the truth, for the coyote is probably the least finicky of any animal about its diet.

The coyote's main foods are rabbits and rodents, but it also eats insects, fish, lizards, frogs, garbage scraps, and porcupines. For dessert, coyotes favor ripe fruit. They will sneak into a farmer's garden at night to sample berries and melons, often taking one bite of every ripe melon!

The coyote is also a scavenger, which means it will eat the bodies of dead animals (known as carrion) when it finds them. Together with vultures and other scavengers, the coyotes help prevent the spread of disease through their efficient disposal of germ-infested carcasses.

During the winter, mice are often on the coyote's menu. To catch these tiny rodents, a coyote will listen for the faint sounds of a mouse squeaking in an air pocket under a snowbank. Then the coyote leaps high in the air, arches its back like a cat, and plunges down through the snow to pluck out the tasty mouse.

HUNTING STRATEGIES ● Coyotes often hunt alone, but they sometimes team up in pairs or small groups. When they hunt as partners, they
use a relay system. One coyote will chase the quarry toward a hiding
spot where its partner lies in wait, ready to take up the hunt afresh.

Acting "loco" is another trick the coyote partners have invented.
After one coyote spots a rabbit or mouse, it will suddenly leap stiff-legged
into the air. Then it may chase its tail wildly or run around in circles.
While the fascinated rabbit stares at the "crazy" coyote's antics, the
second coyote sneaks up and grabs it from behind.

The coyote is even clever enough to hunt with other kinds of animals.
Sometimes, for example, a coyote and a badger (a large weasel) will join
forces. The coyote uses its keen senses to sniff out an occupied gopher
burrow and guards the rear entrance. Then the badger goes to work at
the front entrance with its powerful claws, tunneling downward with
incredible speed. When the animal inside runs out its rear door — pop!
The coyote gobbles it up. Another time, the badger will be the first to
have its dinner.

COYOTES VS FARMERS AND RANCHERS ● Besides the wild animals they hunt, a few coyotes also steal domestic lambs, calves, and chickens. This habit has earned them the hatred of farmers and ranchers, yet the total good that coyotes do far outweighs the bad. The coyotes actually benefit the farmers and ranchers by consuming millions of rodents and insects that are harmful to grasslands and crops.

In areas where the coyote has been eliminated, the result is usually disastrous for the farmers. Their crops are soon overrun by such hordes of insects and rodents that only drastic measures can bring the pests under control. Yet the coyote could have done that same job of pest control much better — and cheaper — than the farmer.

Sheep ranchers began an all-out war against the coyote in the 1930's. At that time, they persuaded the federal government to begin killing coyotes. The government hired hundreds of agents to shoot, trap, and poison these animals on federal lands throughout the West. During the next 40 years, government trappers killed over two million coyotes.

Their deadliest weapon, Compound 1080 poison, was introduced in the 1940's. When this poison was used, much more damage was done than simply eliminating coyotes. Thousands of other innocent animals were killed. Since this poison takes a long time to break down chemically, it has what is called a "chain effect." Even after an animal eats it and dies, the poison is still lethal. Then, if another animal or bird eats the dead animal's body, it will also die from the poison. In one year alone during the 1960's, trappers using 1080 and other poisons killed not only 89,653 coyotes, but also 24,273 foxes, 20,780 lynx and bobcats, 19,052 skunks, 10,078 raccoons, 7,615 opossums, 6,941 badgers, 2,779 wolves, 842 bears, 294 mountain lions, as well as countless eagles and other birds.

In 1972, the government banned the use of poisons on public lands (shooting and trapping are still legal), but ranchers are now putting great pressure on the government to loosen controls. If they are success-ful, the coyote, like the wolf, may vanish from huge areas of its western range. In spite of the many biological studies that have proved the important role this animal plays in controlling rodents and insects, a few self-interested ranchers may determine its fate.

IN SEARCH OF SAFETY ● Because of the extermination campaigns in the West, some coyotes began to migrate in search of safer habitats. Since these animals were extending their range, a few people assumed that the total coyote population was also increasing. But studies showed that in some western states, the number of coyotes had definitely declined.

Meanwhile, during the 1950's in New England, a new wild animal appeared that had never been seen before in that region. It had some characteristics of a wolf, but looked more like a large coyote. At first, some people thought it might be a coy-dog — the offspring of a coyote and a domestic dog. Others believed it was a strain of domestic dog that had become wild.

After much study and debate, scientists agreed that this puzzling creature was actually a new type of coyote — the *eastern* coyote. Its ancestors had migrated east, they believed, to escape the extermination campaigns in its native western states. Once it arrived in the East, the coyote easily moved into the ecological role left vacant when the New England wolves were killed off long before.

AUTHOR'S NOTE • After reading about wolves and coyotes, you may want to have one of these interesting animals as a pet. I must warn you against this idea: Wolves and coyotes should not be kept as pets, for the following reasons.

• These animals are extremely curious and can be very destructive as a result. They might tear open a mattress to find out why it squeaked, or scratch through a rug in search of an intriguing smell.

• Coyotes and wolves are not easily trained. This is true not because they are stupid or slow to learn, but rather because they are very independent. As Dr. Randall Lockwood, an expert on animal communication, has said: "You can train these animals to do anything *they* want to do!"

• Wolves in particular are highly social animals. They should not live as solitary human pets, but should always be together with others of their own kind.

• People who are unfamiliar with wolves and coyotes may be unnecessarily frightened by a pet animal, and serious problems might result. When a wolf first meets a new person, for example, its greeting behavior may seem very rough—though the wolf only means to be friendly. Its greeting might frighten a new acquaintance. If the person then tried to strike the wolf or ran in fear, a very serious situation could result. Incidents like this, in which a person might be frightened or even hurt, could seriously harm the reputation of all wolves and coyotes.

For these and other reasons, most animal experts feel strongly that you won't help wolves or coyotes by keeping one as a pet. The best way to show your love for these animals is not to lock one in your house or yard, but to help the wolves and coyotes living in the wild.

HOW YOU CAN HELP • If you would like to help the wolf and coyote, there are several things you can do. First, you can learn more about these animals and their environments by reading the books available at your library and local bookstores. With your knowledge and awareness, you can help other people understand the truth about these animals and the threats to their survival.

You can also join in the activities of groups that work to protect animals and their habitats. There may be a nature club, zoo, or museum in your area that sponsors such activities. Also, listed below are some national organizations that have been very active in helping wolves and coyotes. If you are interested in any of these groups, write to them for more information.

The Defenders of Wildlife
1244 19th Street, N.W.
Washington, D.C. 20036

KIND, *a youth organization of the Humane Society*
2100 L Street, N.W.
Room 200
Washington, D.C. 20037

W.O.L.F. (Wildlife Orientation Lecture Foundation)
RD 1
Traver Road
Pleasant Valley, New York 12569
(W.O.L.F. is an educational organization that will arrange lectures on wolves for schools and other groups.)

Wild Canid Survival and Research Center (W.C.S.R.C.)
Wolf Sanctuary
P.O. Box 20528
St. Louis, Missouri 63139